THE
SHAKSPERE
COAT-OF-ARMS

AMS PRESS

NEW YORK

THE
SHAKSPERE
COAT-OF-ARMS

DESCRIBED BY

SAML. A. TANNENBAUM

"Report me and my cause aright."
—Hamlet.

PRINTED AND PUBLISHED FOR THE AUTHOR BY
THE TENNY PRESS
NEW YORK
1908

Library of Congress Cataloging in Publication Data

Tannenbaum, Samuel Aaron, 1874?-1948
  The Shakspere coat-of-arms.

  1. Shakespeare, William, 1564-1616—Biography—
Ancestry. 2. Shakespeare family. 3. Heraldry—
Great Britain. I. Title.
PR2901.T3   1974   822.3'3 [B]   71-176453
ISBN 0-404-06336-5

Reprinted from the edition of 1908, New York
First AMS edition published, 1974
Manufactured in the United States of America

AMS PRESS, INC.
New York, N.Y. 10003

Key to colors: In blazonry black (sable) is conventionally represented by a series of vertical lines crossed at right angles by a series of horizontal lines; gold (aurum), by black dots on a white surface; silver (argent), by a white surface.

"We will draw the curtain and show you the picture."
—*Twelfth Night.*

CONTRARY to the opinion of the very eminent literary genius who said that he was very grateful that we know so little of William Shakspere the man, the world at large has for the past century and a half evinced a great and laudable curiosity as to the facts of Shakespere's life. Earnest investigators have applied themselves with matchless zeal to the task of unearthing some new bit of evidence. Cellars, garrets, storehouses and official records in the most out of the way places have been searched. But all more or less in vain. To the professed Shaksperean nothing almost is more amazing than the peculiar fatality which has attended almost everything in any way connected with the history of William Shakspere. Most disastrous chances of moving accidents by flood and field and fire, together with the ravages of time, ignorance and religious bigotry, have wiped away large stores of invaluable documents and books that would have made the life of the "World's Poet" and of his brilliant contemporaries as light as high noon to us. As it is, we know the Elizabethan age—the most wonderful age in England's history—less intimately than the age of Chaucer. Even the grammar of Shakspere's language is less known than Chaucer's.

But, paradoxical as it may sound, our knowledge of the facts of Shakspere's life is chiefly obscured by an excess of documentary evidence and traditions. So that the writing of his biography reduces itself almost to a series of debates, matching tradition against tradition and document against document. In which house was he born? Did he first see the light of day on the 22d or the 23d day of the month? Was his mother one of the daughters of the noble family of Arden descended from Alfred the Great? What was his father's ancestry? Was his (William's) marriage legal? Was his wife Anne Whately or Anne Hathaway? What was his early education? Did he poach on Sir Thomas Lucy's preserves and then lampoon him? Why did he leave Stratford? Was he a butcher's apprentice, a lawyer's clerk, a pedagogue, an apothecary's boy, or what? etc., etc. There is hardly a single fact in his life which is not the subject of dispute, his disciples being divided into different camps even on the subject of the spelling of his name. This condition of affairs is also largely due to the carelessness, ignorance, partisanship or prejudices of his biographers and commentators, some of whom have blindly and unquestioningly followed their predecessors who erred because of the scantiness of evidence, and others of whom have written not with the object of ascertaining the truth, but of proving some theory.

Considering the mass of evidence brought to light by those indefatigable investigators, Malone, Collier and James O. Halliwell-Phillipps, it is almost beyond belief that so simple a matter as the coat-of-arms assigned to John Shakspere in 1596 should be matter of controversy. Did William or John make the application for coat-armor? Did the College of Heraldry grant

the application? When was it granted, in 1596 or 1599? Was the Shakspere family entitled to a coat-of-arms? These and other questions arising from the subject are still matters of debate, but we shall leave them for the present and devote ourselves to a description of the arms.

The inaccuracies in the blazoning of the Shakspere arms in all the biographies of the poet and in the many editions of his works are typical of the carelessness and indifference to truth with which matters concerning Shakspere have been generally treated. This is the more remarkable when we consider the importance which the gentry and nobility at the end of the sixteenth century attached to the subject of coat-armor and how jealously the College of Arms watched any unlawful assumption of arms or the minutest departure from the arms assigned. As a matter of fact charges were brought against William Dethick and the learned Camden for having assigned to Shakspere a shield too closely resembling the Lord Mouley's.

The only works in which the Shakspere arms are not incorrectly depicted are those in which they are not depicted at all, or only in fac-simile of the sketch found in the original drafts preserved in the College of Arms and in photographic reproductions of the Stratford monument. This statement is true, not only of Shakspere biographies and commentaries, but, what is much more remarkable, of the most ambitious and learned works on English Heraldry. Not one of the poet's many commentators —not even the German ones—seems to have thought of consulting a heraldic handbook or glossary, or even a dictionary, for the purpose of ascertaining what the descriptions of the Shakspere arms in the original drafts mean.

In the year 1596—a few months before William purchased
New Place, the largest mansion in Stratford—John Shakspere,
the poet's father, now much advanced in years and relieved of
the burden of supporting his family, applied to the College of
Heraldry in London, of which William Dethick was then the
head, for a coat-of-arms, claiming the coveted privilege on the
grounds that his "parentes and late antecessors" had been advanced and rewarded for valiant and faithful services by King
Henry VII.; that the family had lived in Warwickshire for a long
time in good reputation and credit; that about 1576 Robert
Cook, Clarencieux, had assigned him coat-armor; that he had
been Mayor and Justice of the Peace of Stratford-upon-Avon, an
incorporated town, that he had lands and tenements to the value
of 500 pounds, and that he had married Mary, the daughter
and one of the heirs of Robert Arden of Wilmcote.

It so happens that there have been preserved in the records of
the College two drafts of the intended assignment of arms.   In
the first of these, known as MS. Vincent 157, Art. 23 (repro-
duced in reduced fac-simile in the Miscellanea Genealogica et
Heraldica, 1886, Vol. 1, and in Stephen Tucker's "Assignment of Arms to Shakspere and Arden," London, 1884) a
document that bears all the traces of having been written by one
inexperienced in drawing up heraldic drafts—the arms are thus
described:

"Gould on a bend sable a speare of the first the poynt steeled
proper.   And for his Creast or Cognizance A faulcon his winges
displayed Argent standing on a wrethe of his Coullores supporting
a Speare gould steled as aforesaid sett upon a healmett wth mantelles and tasseles as hath ben accustomed and more playnely ap-
pearethe depicted on the margent."

Fig.· 1

This very intelligible description, leaving out of consideration the erasures and corrections, is further elucidated by a pen-sketch of the shield and crest, without the helmet and mantle, however, in the upper left hand margin of the draft. (Fig. 1.) It is worthy of note that in this rough sketch the colors of the falcon, the spear, the spear-point and the wreath are not indicated, and that the motto (which is not mentioned in the body of either draft), Non Sans Droict, appears twice above the crest, each time incorrectly.

In the second draft (MS. Vincent 157, Art. 24), a later, slightly altered, corrected, fuller and, in some respects, more specific version of the former document, the arms are thus blazoned:

"Gould on a Bend Sables a Speare of the first steeled argent. And for his Creast or Cognizance a falcon his winges displayed Argent standing on a wrethe of his Coullors supporting A Speare Gould Steeled as aforesaid sett vppo' a helmett wth mantelles & tasseles as hathe ben accustomed and dothe more playnely appeare depicted on this margent."

In the pen-sketch accompanying this description the colors and tinctures of the different parts of the shield and crest are fully and correctly indicated (Fig. 2). It is pleasant to speculate—and the speculation is not wholly unsupported by evidence —that the great William himself, the world's idol, had a hand in the drafting of this document. Some corroboration of this conjecture is found in the recently discovered proof that the poet was an expert in matters pertaining to heraldry, and was employed by the nobility to devise patterns of arms for them.

Fig. 2.

Unquestionably one of the most interesting documents relative to William Shakspere extant is the so-called heraldic draft of

1599 known as "MS. College of Arms, R. 21." It is no less than a proposal to permit John Shakspere to impale (i. e., to combine) the illustrious arms of the Ardens of Warwickshire, descended from King Alfred, with his own. There is every reason to believe that for some reason, probably because of inability to prove the connnection of William's mother with those Ardens, or possibly because of the noted Catholicism of the Ardens—Sir Edward Arden, Sheriff of the county, had been executed in 1583 for conspiring against the life of the Queen—this privilege was not granted by the College. In this rough draft the armorial bearings are thus described:

"In a field of Gould vppon A Bond Sables A Speare of the first the Poynt vpward hedded Argent And for his Creast or Cognizance A ffalcon wth his wynges desplayed standing on A wrethe of his Coullors Supporting A Speare Armed hedded or & steeled Sylver fyxed vppon A helmet wth mantelles & tasselles as more playnely maye appeare depicted on this Margent."

It is to be noted that the color of the wings is not given, and that the limning of the spear in the crest is almost unintelligible. The drawing that accompanies the description is not without its errors. The spear in the crest is marked with the letter "s" (sable-black) instead of with the letters "or" (gold), and the wings of the falcon are marked "or" instead of "ar" (argentum-silver). (Fig. 3.)

Fig. 3

In the Index College of Arms the following description of the arms is found: "O on a/S. a Spear. O. Crest a Falcon, wings display'd, A. supporting a Spear in 1. O. Granted 20 October, 1596." This may be thus interpreted: "Or, on a Bend sable a Spear Or. Crest a Falcon, wings displayed, Argent, supporting a Spear in pale Or." Nothing is said of the color of the spear's point, nor of the helmet and tassels.

A comparison of the descriptions in the three drafts and in the Index leaves absolutely no room for doubt that the arms which the College granted or intended to grant John Shakspere were these: "Or, on a Bend Sable a Spear of the first, the point Argent, and for the Crest a Falcon, Argent, with his wings displayed, supporting a Spear in pale, Or, the point upward headed, Argent, standing on a wreath of his colors and provided with a mantle and tassels."

Notwithstanding the abundance and the authenticity, as well as the accessibility, of the testimony, John Guillim, the Father of

Heraldry, in his "Display of Heraldrie" (ed. 1724, the earliest edition to which we have had access) says: "Shakespear, Or, on a Bend Sable, a Tilting Spear of the Field is born by the Name of Shakespear, and was given by William Dethick Garter, to William (sic) Shakespear the renowned Poet." Nothing is said of the crest and of the point of the spear. Bad as this is it compares very favorably with the following from the "Encyclopedia Heraldica:" "Or, on a bend sa. a spear of the first.—Crest, a falcon, displayed, ppr. holding a spear or. (Monumental inscription, to the immortal Shakspeare, in Stratford-upon-Avon Church, Warwickshire, ob. 6th August, 1628.)" And we can safely judge of the value of Victor Hugo's "Life of Shakespeare" by his description of the arms: "The family had for coat-of-arms an arm holding a lance—allusive arms, which were confirmed, they say, by Queen Elizabeth in 1595, and apparent, at the time we write, on Shakespeare's tomb." In extenuation of Victor Hugo it may be said that he was writing while in exile, far removed from a public library. But what can possibly be said in extenuation of that host of eighteenth century scholars and critics who were duped by the young Ireland, whose drawing of the Shakspere crest should alone have been sufficient to betray the forged character of his newly discovered documents?

We are now prepared to define the various heraldic terms occurring in the ancient descriptions of the Shakspere arms:

"Or."—Gold. As used above it means a conventional shield having a golden surface, conventionally represented by black dots on a white surface.

"Bend Sable."—A black belt or band of about one-third the area of the shield extending diagonally from the upper right-hand corner of the shield downward and to the left to the opposite side of the shield near its base.

"Spear of the first."—A tilting-spear with a funnel-shaped projection (the vamplate) over the handle, of the color first mentioned in the description.

"Argent."—Silver, conventionally represented by a white surface.

"Crest."—A figure placed above the shield and helmet, standing on a wreath. A very important part of the arms.

"Wings displayed."—Both wings of the falcon expanded and directed somewhat upwards. When the wings are open and pointing down they are said to be "disclosed." When the wings are reversed, with the tips drooping, they are said to be "inverted." When both wings are raised vertically and thrown back so as almost to touch each other they are said to be "erect." "A falcon with wings displayed" is quite different from a "falcon displayed."

"Helmet."—This must, in the arms of a "gentleman," be of steel, but it may be enriched with gold. A mere gentleman's helmet must be represented in profile, with visor closed. It rests directly on the shield.

"Wreath."—A twisted band composed of two strands of silk representing alternately the principal metal and the principal tincture in the arms. When properly represented it shows six divisions or twists. It is placed on the helmet and supports the crest.

"Cognizance."—A heraldic device, similar to the crest, worn on the liveries of followers, on banners, ensigns, etc.

"Proper."—This term means that the figure or device mentioned is to be shown as having its natural shape or color, or its conventional shape or color.

"Mantle and tassels."—An artistic conventional representation of a mantle or cloak investing the helmet and shield, which is intended to make the coat-of-arms prominent. It should be of the principal color and metal of the arms.

"In pale."—This phrase is equivalent to "upward headed," and means "borne vertically."

"Steeled."—This word, as used above, can mean only that the point of the lance was to be of steel, and, therefore, to be represented as white. It does not mean that the spear was to have no head.

"Armed."—This was said of the heads of arrows, spears, etc., when these were different in tincture from the rest of the bearing.

The phrase "as hath been accustomed," as used in the above descriptions, can mean only "as is customary in coats-of-arms," although it may have been intended for "as John Shakspere had been accustomed to display them."

Fig. 4

With the aid of these definitions we may now translate our heraldic formula of the Shakspere arms as follows: "A golden

silver-headed tilting-spear, pointing upwards, within a broad black band in a golden shield, the band extending from the upper right-hand corner of the field down and to the left. Above the shield and resting on it is a silver and gold helmet in profile, with visor closed, supporting a gold and silver wreath of six convolutions, the helmet and shield being invested with a gold and silver mantle with golden tassels. Resting on the wreath is a white falcon with both wings spread and pointing upwards, supporting in one claw a silver-headed golden spear pointing upwards. Above the timbre or crest is a scroll bearing the motto, "Non Sans Droict." (Fig. 4.)

The most common errors in previous depictions of these arms —one or more of which occurs in all—are these: A black shield; a black shield spotted with gold; a bend or; a golden or a sable lance; a golden helmet or none at all; a golden mantle or none at all; no tassels; a golden wreath, or a sable wreath, or a wreath of only five twists; a golden falcon supporting a golden lance; and, almost universally, the falcon's wings pointing down, i. e., inverted, disclosed, or conjoined in lure. One has only to look at the back or covers of almost any work on Shakspere—even on that monument of American scholarship, the Furness Variorum— to see these errors illustrated.

The canting or punning nature of the charges in the Shakspere arms, as well as the importance of the term "displayed," is so well brought out by Fleay (Shakespeare Manual, p. 311) that we cannot do better than to quote him. He says: "Here is the spear plain enough, but where is the shake? In the words 'a falcon with his wings displayed,' I think. For how could the name, or rather this part of the name, be expressed in the

charge? There is no means of representing shake but by something shaking, and no inorganic thing can be so drawn; nor among living creatures can I find anything that can represent shaking excepting a bird shaking its wings previously to flying, which can heraldically be expressed. The connection between shaking and 'with wings displayed' may be gathered from the following considerations: Lady Juliana Berners, in her work on Hawking, especially warns her readers never to say of a falcon that she shakes, but always to say 'she rouses.' And in accordance with this, a bird shaking its wings in preparation to fly, that is to say, with wings displayed,' was often blazoned in the heraldic books as rousant. If we refer to the old dictionaries we find this confirmed. For instance, in Ryder's Latin Dictionary to rouse is translated "corusco," and in referring to "corusco" we find 'Corusco, pallo kradaino, vibro, oculorum aciem perstringo. To shine, glisten or lighten. To brandish, c. gladium vel hastam, Virg. to brandish or shake.' So that the very word used by our ancestors in Latin to express the shaking of a spear was also used by them for the displaying the wings in heraldry."

It is one of those ironies of fate that he who was assigned the motto "Non Sans Droict" should have his right to arms challenged and his integrity in the matter impeached by biographers living three hundred years after him who do not take the pains to investigate the matter.

As to the falcon in the Shakspere arms, G. R. French has called attention to the fact (Shakespeareana Genealogica, p. 523)

that the falcon was one of the badges of Edward IV., father-in-law of Henry VII. (he who the Shaksperes said had advanced and rewarded their "antecessors" for valiant services) and that no person would have ventured to adopt it for his crest without special favor.

Such was the eternal blazon assigned to Shakspere in commemoration of the valiant feats of his ancestors. Were it left for us to assign his arms we should substitute a pen for the spear as a symbol of that enchanting quill that won him undying fame and immortalized our English tongue.